HEIFETZ *Collection*

LA RONDE DES LUTINS *(Dance of the Goblins)*
for Violin and Piano

ANTONIO BAZZINI, Op. 25

Critical Urtext Edition

Edited by Endre Granat

KEISER®

LA RONDE DES LUTINS
(Dance of the Goblins)
for Violin and Piano

ANTONIO BAZZINI, Op. 25

2

168

176

184
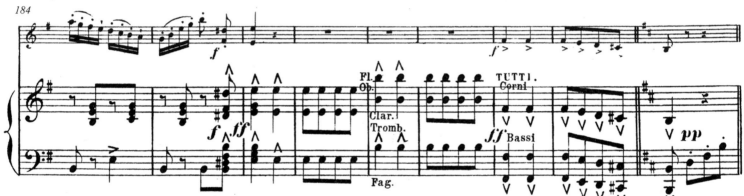

193

202

SOUTHERN MUSIC FLUTE WORKS
SELECTED FLUTE EDITIONS/ ARRANGEMENTS

COLLECTIONS

Nancy Andrews
Paris Conservatory Album: 16 Short Lyric Pieces — B579 - HL240976

Gilbert and Sullivan, arr. Galway/ Overton
Arias for Flute and Piano — B577 - HL240978
Arias for Flute Choir — B583 - HL240979
Arias for Two Flutes and Piano — B584 - HL240981

SOLOS (with piano accompaniment unless otherwise stated)

Giulio Briccialdi, arr. Sir James Galway
The Carnival of Venice (Il Carnevale di Venezia) — SU797 - HL240977

Eugene Magalif
For Tanya (opt. Flute 2 and Wind Chimes) — SU810 - HL244914

Eugene Magalif
Romance — SU811 - HL244916

Eugene Magalif
Revelation — SU809 - HL244915

Jules Mouquet, ed. Sir James Galway
La Flute de Pan — SU804 - HL240982

Johann Quantz, ed. Sir James Galway
Concerto in G Major — SU805 - HL240983

M.A. Reichert, arr. Sir James Galway
The Encore Solo (unaccompanied) — SU794 - HL240984

Paul Taffanel, ed. Sir James Galway
Grand Fantasy on Mignon — SU795 - HL240985

Paul Wetzger, arr. Sir James Galway
Am Waldesbach (By the Forest Brook), Op. 33 — SU798 - HL240986

Charles-Marie Widor, ed. Sir James Galway
Suite — SU803 - HL240987

Southern MUSIC
EXCLUSIVELY DISTRIBUTED BY
HAL•LEONARD®

keisersouthernmusic.com
Questions/ comments? info@southernmusic.com

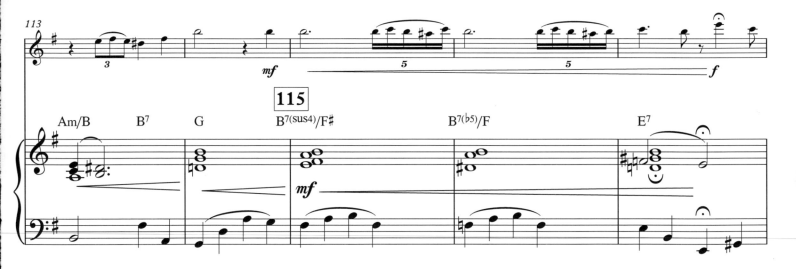

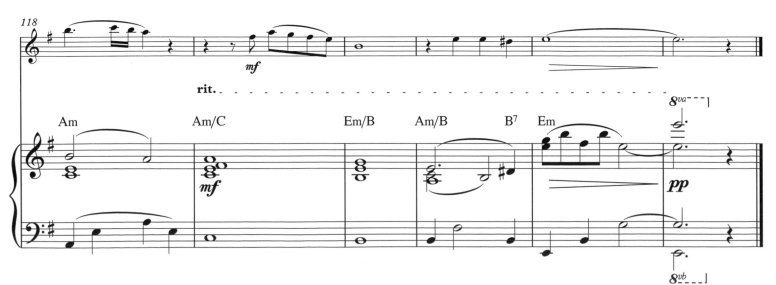

6

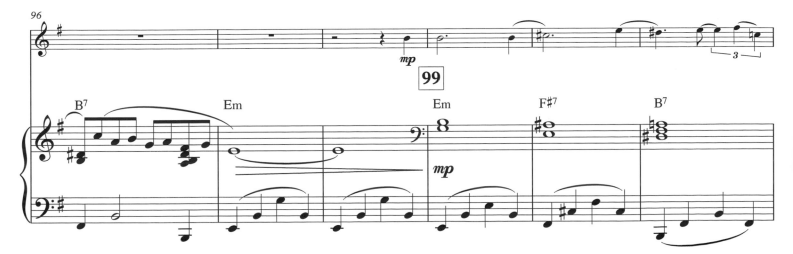

SU811

SOUTHERN MUSIC FLUTE WORKS
SELECTED FLUTE EDITIONS/ ARRANGEMENTS

COLLECTIONS

Nancy Andrews
Paris Conservatory Album: 16 Short Lyric Pieces   B579 - HL240976
Gilbert and Sullivan, arr. Galway/ Overton
Arias for Flute and Piano   B577 - HL240978
Arias for Flute Choir   B583 - HL240979
Arias for Two Flutes and Piano   B584 - HL240981

SOLOS (with piano accompaniment unless otherwise stated)

Giulio Briccialdi, arr. Sir James Galway
The Carnival of Venice (Il Carnevale di Venezia)   SU797 - HL240977
Eugene Magalif
For Tanya (opt. Flute 2 and Wind Chimes)   SU810 - HL244914
Eugene Magalif
Romance   SU811 - HL244916
Eugene Magalif
Revelation   SU809 - HL244915
Jules Mouquet, ed. Sir James Galway
La Flute de Pan   SU804 - HL240982
Johann Quantz, ed. Sir James Galway
Concerto in G Major   SU805 - HL240983
M.A. Reichert, arr. Sir James Galway
The Encore Solo (unaccompanied)   SU794 - HL240984
Paul Taffanel, ed. Sir James Galway
Grand Fantasy on Mignon   SU795 - HL240985
Paul Wetzger, arr. Sir James Galway
Am Waldesbach (By the Forest Brook), Op. 33   SU798 - HL240986
Charles-Marie Widor, ed. Sir James Galway
Suite   SU803 - HL240987

Southern
MUSIC
EXCLUSIVELY DISTRIBUTED BY
Hal•Leonard®

keisersouthernmusic.com
Questions/ comments? info@southernmusic.com

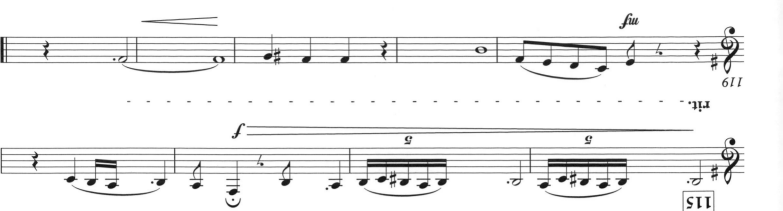

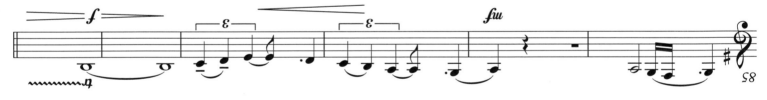

Flute

3

Flute

To Rita D'Arcangelo
ROMANCE

Eugene Magalif,
ASCAP

Ballad ♩ =116

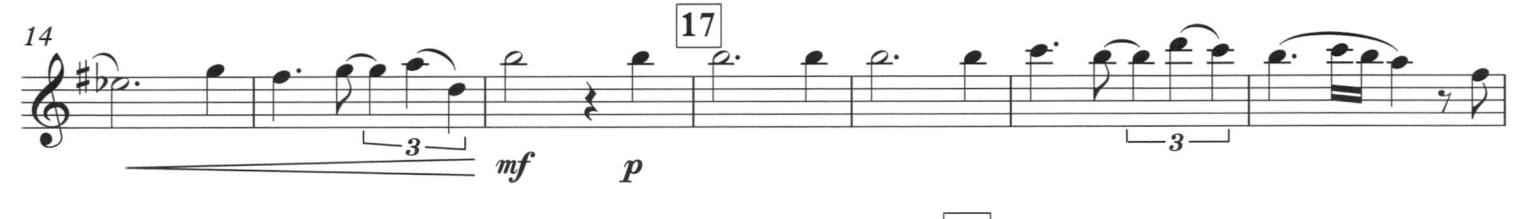

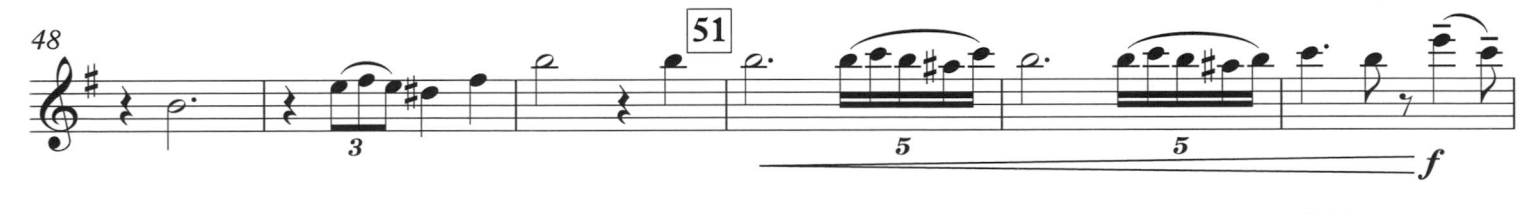

Eugene MAGALIF

Romance
for Flute and Piano

_____

To Rita D'Arcangelo

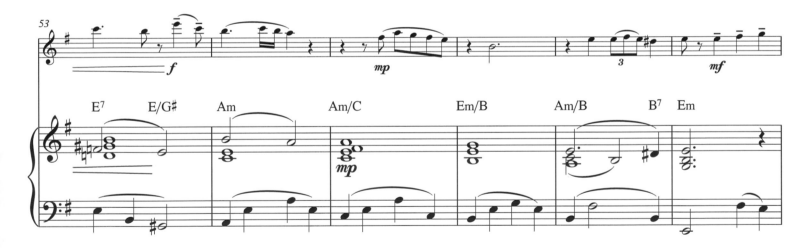

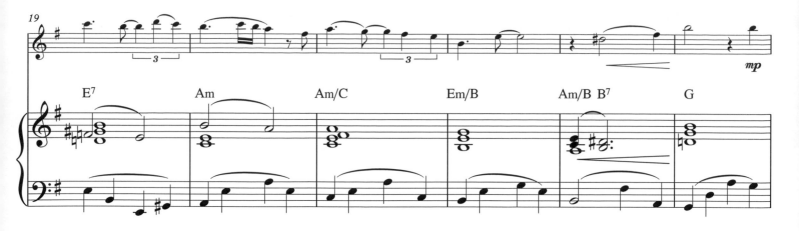

To Rita D'Arcangelo

ROMANCE

Eugene Magalif,
ASCAP